Rhyme
and
Reason

by
Denise Shaw

A CIP catalogue record for this book is available from the
British Library.

ISBN 978-1-84436-755-9

CLASSIFICATION: POETRY

Printed and bound in Great Britain.
First published in Great Britain in 2008 by
United Press Ltd
Admail 3735
London
EC1B 1JB
Tel: 0870 240 6190
Fax: 0870 240 6191
All Rights Reserved

Paper used in the production of books published by
United Press comes only from sustainable forests.

www.unitedpress.co.uk

On the fourth day of July 1952, I was born in Halifax, but shortly after my birth my Father was appointed chauffeur-gardener for Miss Fitzwilliam at Slingsby Hall, on the Fitzwilliam Estate, and so my family and I moved to Slingsby near Castle Howard, North Yorkshire.

My loving and idyllic childhood was to mould me for my adult years to come. My husband, Stephen, and my now grown up twin sons and daughter, have been a constant support. My love of the countryside, nature, wildlife, and animals coupled with my respect for fairness and good manners, have influenced my style of writing.

Denise Shaw

CONTENTS

YORKSHIRE AIR AMBULANCE

I was born in Yorkshire, I'm Yorkshire through and
through, and proud of our Air Ambulance and everything
they do.
Life's not always simple and often things go wrong,
accidents will happen when danger comes along.
Time is of the essence, when things are looking bad, if we
had an accident, of them we would be glad.
Will we need the Ambulance? Of that we'll never know.
When human life hangs in there, by road is far too slow!
That's when we need Ambulance, the one that's in the
sky, because we have this service, more people will not
die.
Come on then Yorkshire people, let's raise the funds
agen, remember (if thou gets owt for nowt, get it for thy
sen.)

THE GREAT NORTH RUN

Just thirteen miles to go, I thought while standing at the
start, my Yorkshire pride runs through my veins and
pumping to my heart.
I started running late in life, but better late than never.
At the end of my first race I was feeling rather cleaver.
There I was, all kitted out in my Nike trainers and people
running by my side were people that were famous.
This run, it is my last one, my knees have really had it.
Six red arrows fly overhead, I'm feeling patriotic.
Running down the final mile, my feet are bruised and
battered.
I'm out of puff, I'm feeling sick and oh, my legs are shat-
tered.
My days are numbered on the roads, maybe I'll take up
writing.
If it is to be my last, then I will go down fighting.

4

A FATHER'S QUEST

Father standing with a shotgun outside the young lad's
door.
Come out and face the music, come see what I've in
store.
It appears you know my daughter, a very pretty sight.
She listened not to my advice, she didn't dance all night.
She's in a spot of bother, we'll solve it very soon, be at
the church by 2 o'clock on Sunday afternoon.
I've been and booked the vicar, the organist and choir.
There's one thing left for me to know, your name I will
require.
Now all things considered, and not thinking of yourself,
this means my dearest daughter will be left not on the
shelf.

MY FAVOURITE DAY

Sunday is my favourite day, with all my family round,
the laughter and the chitchat is such a lovely sound.
The roast is in the oven, the smell, a crowd, would stop,
the Yorkshire pudding's in full bloom, stuck to the oven
top.
We sit around the table and eat until we burst, "Leave
room for homemade apple pie," so who's to be the first?
We wobble round the fire and slumber into sleep,
everyone except for me, at my family I will peep.
This moment I will cherish, as we are all together, I'm
tempted to lock all the doors and keep them here forever.

A CHOSEN CHILD

One dark, dreary morning, the 4th July, I came into this world, a soft muffled cry.

My mother did not want me, my Father the same, he had a wife, so who was to blame.

She had to think quickly, what could be her option - the child that she had would go for adoption.

That was the first day that God stood by me, he chose Ken and Marge for my parents to be, if not for them, I'd have been quite alone.

Oh no, said Ken, we'll bring her up as our own.

They fattened me up and dressed me in pink, they had everything sorted before you could blink.

They gave me so much, they spoiled me to death; faced with the choice, they'd give me their last breath.

The support that they gave me is so hard to measure, the memories of them through life I will treasure.

They taught me to give as well as receive, to be kind, to be honest and always believe, to do unto others as you would do too and always spare time, regardless of who.

My parents were special and incredibily kind to have some better impossible to find.

I hope as a parent I've been half as good and remembered their words as best as I could.

They are both now in heaven with God by their side, as they were my parents, he was their guide.

When I look at the stars and they look down on me, I hope Ken and Marge will be so proud of me.

My life was decided that July day, her feelings who knows as she gave me away?

My thanks go to her for the decision she made, my life would be different had she kept me and stayed.

THE PRIMARY TEACHER

Her job as a teacher goes on and on, she's all things
rolled into one.

From the very first day her objective is burning, to be
sure that her pupils are hungry for learning.

There's reading and writing and just a few sums and time
to play out when lunchtime comes.

The classroom seems big and the teacher looks tall,
assembly is daunting when sat in the hall.

When her pupils respond and their potential is clear, it
reminds her just why she chose this career.

Foundations aren't built from mortar alone, they need
strength and stability equal to stone.

Her job feels well done when she hears the say, we'll
come back tomorrow and then every day.

THE STRIPPER

I've got this thing going with a stripper, we've been joined
at the hip for a while, he's big and he's hot and he's
steamy, and I'm telling you he's got some style.
Positions not yet invented, by now you'll be getting the
jist, my neck's on a piece of elastic and I feel like a con-
tortionist.
He's proving to be quite a handful, have I bitten off more
than to chew?
I know by now what you're thinking and wishing that he
was with you.
Before you jump to conclusion and steel him and hold me
to ransom, I've been stripping the walls down at my
place, with a machine that I hire from Banston.

NEVER GIVE UP

Never give up, never give in, I'm not learning to drive, I'm trying to slim.
I'm finding it hard and I'm not in the mood, this lark's not for me for I like my food.
The thought of hot toast with stacks of Lurpak,
I;m finding it hard, I'll not get the knack.
I'm finding it hard and I'm not a glutton, so I'll go for broke and open my button.
There is only one way I'll not come unstuck, I'll just have to face it, my jaw wired up!

THE EYES

It's all in the eyes, they eyes have it all, and in the absence of sound, they speak volumes to all.
When silence prevails, look deep and you'll see,
the presence of sadness and the need to be free.
When spirits are broken and feelings despair, it's all in the eyes, the eyes have it there.
When darkness is lifted and spirits ignite, the eyes appear open focused and bright.
Words fail to explain, no matter how small, you don't have to say anything as the eyes say it all.

THE DRUG

This drug is not new, it's been around forever, some people use it, some people never.
Once you get the taste for what it is in store, take it from me, you'll be back for more.
It makes you feel good, it makes you stand tall, I've been hopelessly addicted since I was small.
This drug will not kill you, it has the reverse.
It's not bought at the chemist or given by nurse.
Do something for others without personal gain, the high that this gives you is more than cocaine.
By now you'll be thinking and trying to guess the name of this drug, it's called Selflessness!

8

MARY AGNESS

There is a disease that could be contagious, to help, stop
the spread, you would be courageous. Young lives are
destroyed by the strain of this thing, it's not Aids or
Cancer, it's called BULLYING. Good and successful are
always the victim, the bullies are jealous, so that's why
they pick them.

Yes, she was different and not like the rest, she is good
and she's kind and was one of the best. While she was at
school she hoped to be mentioned, her soul was pure
and theirs were tormented. I sat hour upon hour just
hearing her cry, her heart was broken, I thought she
would die.

Her journey's been long and filled with despair, so I gave
her my heart, my love and my care. She battled long and
hard, but she had it to do, it was short of a miracle she
ever came through.

Their day of judgement is surely to come and they will
have to answer for what they have done. If you are a
bully and you know who you are, as you go through your
life you won't get very far. You are to be pitted, have no
conscience and weak, you are inadequate people, just
attention you seek. In your life something's missing that
your victims possess, inner peace, love and kindness and
true happiness.

As she leaves university with her degree, the bullies will
be thinking, I wish that were me. She's successful and
happy and her new life has begun, to the bullies, you
have lost, your victim has won.

We must break the cycle and stop all the pain, or the
bullies will bully again and again! Please understand that
bullying is not cool, I am the mother of that child that
was bullied in school

CHARLIE MOON

While in the borough market on Friday afternoon,
I bumped into an old friend, his name was Charlie Moon.
We stopped a while, we chewed the fat and caught up on
our life.
Just before he left me he said he'd lost his wife, to that I
said, shout very loud, she's sure to hear your cry.
"No, I did not lose her here, I buried her last July."

TOMORROW'S THE DAY

Tomorrow's the day, the day of the sales.
I'll be there first light, come rain or high gales.
I cannot miss out on that little black dress I've wanted
for ages, I'll take nothing less.
I'll have four inch heels and jewellry to match and a hint
of Chanel, I'll be quite a catch.
As I sit here and ponder, it's not what it seems, I have to
admit it's all in my dreams.
I'll buy the tweed skirt, the blouse and the beads, the
hush puppy shoes, they're more to my needs.
Yes, tomorrow's the day, but not to the sales, it's the
sixty and over day out in the Dales.

A WARNING!

Parking my car down at Laurel in front of the garage
doors, then along comes a man in a white van who won't
admit to the damage he's caused.
He said it's all about bonus, I'll lose it if you get your
way, be a man, stand up and be honest, if it means a
dock in your pay.
A warning to you, Joseph Public, his white van's the size
of a barge, so lock up your cars, dive for cover, this white
van is still out at large.

10

IT'S A MAD, MAD WORLD

The world is so fast, when will it all end?
It's no longer a letter, but an e-mail we send.
In this world of high-tech, where the sounds are high
pitch and everything's there at the flick of a switch.
When shopping's online, not a line at the shop and
people just spend and don't ever stop.
Once it was coffee, it was Nescafé, the posh version now
is called a latté.
When stag and hen nights were just a small do, now it's
expected a week in Corfu.
When the going got tough, the tough just got hard, now
it's resolved with a flexible card.
When people were tired from working all day, they just
kept on working till Friday payday.
Times may have changed, good values should not;
it's rewarding to say I am happy with my lot.

THE DENTIST

I have a date with the dentist on Friday at noon,
I'll be there on time, but I won't be there soon.
I'm shaking inside at the thought of the drilling,
If it wasn't for toothache, I'd pass on the filling.
I cannot forget the way that I'm feeling,
So I'll just think of England and stare at the ceiling.
Things could be worse, much worse by far,
The thought of my teeth sitting there in a jar.

REMEMBER WHEN

People do the strangest things, it's called set in their ways.
Why do they do the things they do on designated days?
Monday's always washing day when the creel is pulled up
higher, if the weather's cold and wet they dry them round
the fire.
Tuesday is for ironing, if the washing's dry or not, it's only
for the ironing, not the washing they forgot.
Wednesday's for the windows, they get a right good do, the
steps, the flags, the windowsills and then the outside loo.
Thursday is the bedrooms, they get a thorough clean,
wardrobe tops and skirting boards and places never seen.
Friday is the sitting room, with furniture pulled out, this
is an inconvenience for grandad with the gout.
Saturday was shopping day and what a hefty task, every
stall they went to, is it cheap? Is what they would ask.
Sunday is rest and church day, when the girls might meet
a bloke, one thing is for certain,
there's nowt so queer as folk!

GOD'S TINY CREATURES

In the heart of the wood in the base of a tree, they made a
new house for their family to be
Mum said to Dad, it has to be warm, free from all draught
and safe from all harm.
The day had arrived for the mother to be, Dad went into
shock when he saw there were three,
The babies, all boys, Tom, Dick and Harry, would now
pose a problem for mother to carry.
Dad solved the problem with the aid of a sack; throw them
over your shoulder and on to your back!
As time went by, their family had grown so much, that the
walls had started to moan.
Mum said to Dad, don't worry, don't fear, we'll get them
some bunk beds, the ones from Ikea.

12

SCHOOL DINNERS

I never liked school dinners, and yes I really tried.
They never let me off the hook, despite the fact I cried.
The soggy mashed potatoes with eyes as big as mine
And pies to sink a battle ship, at that I draw the line.
When there was a power cut, the kids would laugh and howl,
But soon the laughter turned to tears when custard is served by trowel.
Have a try of everything, was the order of the day.
I'd stuff it in my pocket, quickly, as she walked away.
Next time she walks towards me, I know just what to do.
I'll try and stall her for a while, till Bunter's had my stew.
There's just one thing I wish for, can you guess who?
His name is Jamie Oliver, his mission is Rescue!

OH, TO BE ON THE CHECKOUT

I work upon the checkout, a job I seldom dread.
But when it comes to end of term, I wished I'd stayed in bed.
The kids around aged nine or ten, standing with a fag,
The other kids around the back, attached to a plastic bag.
They're in and out, their pockets full, they never fail to fill.
The kids are loud, they are on form and swinging from the trolley,
Their mother shouts, you little sods, and whacks them with her brolly.
They hang around the entrance and soon the crowd has grown,
All they ever seem to do is text by mobile phone.
I've seen it all, there is no shock and no, I've not been lead,
But when it comes to end of term, I wished I'd stayed in bed!

13

NEIGHBOURHOOD WATCH

We looked out of our window at our neighbour straight
across, he's always been the under dog, she's always
been the boss.
Our eyes were drawn to something hanging from the bar.
"Oh, my goodness, it's Patrick," this time she's gone too
far.
We rubbed our eyes and looked again and hoped no one
had seen us,
And there on a hanger from the curtain rail was his suit,
back from the cleaners.

ORGANISED

I thought that I was organised, but now I know I'm
not.The list is getting longer of the things that I forgot.
Did I turn the oven on? I'd better go and see. I hope I
turned the oven on, or it's sandwiches for tea.
When it comes to detail, I know just where it's at.
I left the lights on the car and now the battery's flat.
I sorted all the washing, the things I had to do, then I left
a sock in and all the whites went blue.
I always make a shopping list or something of that sort,
but as I put the things away, I forgot more than I bought.
I like to think I'm organised, but reading this, you've
guessed our home it is a happy place, but chaos at its
best!

LONELINESS

Like a cut that won't heal, like a festering sore and the
pain in your heart feels like nothing before.
When day feels like night and night never ends,
When your family's not there and the absence of friends.
When everything's still, though the world turns around
and in bustling crowds, you don't hear a sound.
To be next to a stranger and smile at them only,
It's a cry from within that says, I am lonely.

TWO HEARTS

Two hearts that began as one from the start, separately
beating, but never apart.
That snow-speckled morning would be like no other, two
tiny young lives, today I'm a mother.
The feeling to hold them so close to my skin, the need to
protect them was raging within.
I lay in the darkness and watch daybreak, two tiny
hearts beating, their lives are at stake.
This feeling so strong, it's just like no other, I guess it's
because today I'm a mother.
Ten tiny fingers, ten tiny toes, four big brown eyes, two
button like nose.
A few months ago I would never have guessed that now
I'd be thinking, I've been truly blessed.
Whatever I thought, it's now life begins, life wont be the
same now that I have twins.

SET AN EXAMPLE

Say hello to the person who's passing your way, that one
little word could brighten their day.
Stand up on the bus for a mother to be, and set an
example for others to see.
Hold open the door and let them, walk through, they just
might remember and do the same too.
If you know something's wrong, hold back, don't go
there, be kind and be honest and show that you care.
We may not change the world from corruption and lies,
but failures for certain if nobody tries.

IT'S A DOGS LIFE

It really is a dog's life, but it could have been much
worse. She treats us just like children and expects us to
converse.
We remember please and thank you and guard just like
a hawk, we do not need a potty, but struggle with a knife
and fork.
When walking there's confusion, it really is absurd, is it
dogs or is it children that should be seen and not be
heard.
When the nights upon us everything is dark, if we need
our mother, should we cry or should we bark?
Some dogs have a kennel, others sleep under willow, me
and my brother Alfie have a quilt and a heart shaped pil-
low.
We really love our mother, of that there is no question,
but to tell her that, we are just dogs, not a hint of a
suggestion.